P9-DND-572

Who Was

Maurice Sendak?

RIDGEFIELD LIBRARY
472 MAIN STREET
RIDGEFIELD, CT 06877
(203) 438-2282
www.ridgefieldlibrary.org

**JAN 24
2020**

Who Was Maurice Sendak?

By Janet B. Pascal

Illustrated by Stephen Marchesi

Grosset & Dunlap
An Imprint of Penguin Group (USA) Inc.

To Daddie, who sings me the Queen of the Night's arias from
The Magic Flute. Maurice Sendak would approve—JBP

Grosset & Dunlap
Published by the Penguin Group
Penguin Group (USA) Inc., 375 Hudson Street, New York, New York 10014, USA

USA | Canada | UK | Ireland | Australia | New Zealand | India | South Africa | China
Penguin Books Ltd, Registered Offices: 80 Strand, London WC2R 0RL, England

For more information about the Penguin Group visit penguin.com

If you purchased this book without a cover, you should be aware that this book is stolen
property. It was reported as "unsold and destroyed" to the publisher, and neither the author
nor the publisher has received any payment for this "stripped book."

All rights reserved. No part of this book may be reproduced, scanned, or distributed
in any printed or electronic form without permission. Please do not participate in or
encourage piracy of copyrighted materials in violation of the author's rights.
Purchase only authorized editions.

The publisher does not have any control over and does not assume any responsibility for
author or third-party websites or their content.

Text copyright © 2013 by Janet B. Pascal. Illustrations copyright © 2013 by Stephen
Marchesi. Cover illustration © 2013 by Nancy Harrison. Published by Grosset and Dunlap,
a division of Penguin Young Readers Group, 345 Hudson Street, New York, New York
10014. GROSSET AND DUNLAP is a trademark of Penguin Group (USA) Inc.
Printed in the U.S.A.

Library of Congress Cataloging-in-Publication Data is available.

ISBN 978-0-448-46500-5 (pbk)   10 9 8 7 6 5 4 3 2 1
ISBN 978-0-448-46586-9 (hc)   10 9 8 7 6 5 4 3 2 1

Contents

Who Was
Maurice Sendak?

In 1963, a children's book called *Where the Wild Things Are* was published. It was very different from earlier picture books. Some adults worried that it would frighten children. The Wild Things are monsters with sharp teeth who threaten to eat Max, the hero of the story. Other adults believed the book offered a bad message. Most children's books in the sixties tried to teach children to be good. In this book Max yells at his mother and is sent to his room. But instead of being taught a lesson, he goes off on a splendid adventure and becomes the king of the Wild Things. Not only does he never say he's sorry, he *isn't* sorry.

Today *Where the Wild Things Are* is a classic. Its author, Maurice Sendak, won all the highest honors for writing children's books. For three years, American president Barack Obama chose *Where the Wild Things Are* as the book to be read aloud to children at the White House Easter Egg Roll. "I love this book," he told the kids. When the president growled along with the Wild Things, the Obamas' dog, Bo, started to howl along, too.

Maurice Sendak knew that it wouldn't hurt children to read about his scary Wild Things. Even as a small child, he knew that the world was full of monsters. The only way to deal with them was to do what Max did—stare them in the eyes and show them who was boss. It didn't help to pretend monsters weren't there. "Grown-ups always say they protect their children," he explained to Bernard Holland of the *New York Times*, "but they're really protecting themselves. Besides, you can't protect children. They know everything."

Chapter 1
Looking Out Windows

Maurice Sendak was born on June 10, 1928, into two worlds at once. He lived with his family in Brooklyn, New York. There he ran wild with the gang of children on his block. He went to see movies like *The Wizard of Oz* and Walt Disney's *Pinocchio*. And he read all the comic books he could get his hands on. On special occasions, he crossed the river from Brooklyn into Manhattan, with its skyscrapers, bright lights, and flashing signs.

But just as real to him was the world that his
parents, Philip and Sadie, came from. They were
both born in Poland, in little Jewish villages called
shtetls. His father loved to tell stories from the old
country. There were scary legends about demons,
graveyards, and children who got lost in the forest
and died. Sometimes his father took stories from
the Bible and changed them to make them more
exciting. Maurice got in trouble when he retold
these stories at school.

SHTETLS

SHTETL IS YIDDISH FOR "LITTLE TOWN." THE *SHTETLS* OF EASTERN EUROPE WERE CLOSE-KNIT JEWISH VILLAGES. EVEN IN THE TWENTIETH CENTURY, THE PEOPLE STILL LIVED MUCH THE WAY THEIR ANCESTORS HAD. THEY KEPT FARM ANIMALS FOR FOOD, SO GOATS, DUCKS, AND CHICKENS RAN AROUND ON THE DUSTY ROADS. MOST PEOPLE WORKED AS TRADESMEN OR CRAFTSMEN—SHOPKEEPERS, COBBLERS, TAILORS. THE MOST IMPORTANT PEOPLE IN THE VILLAGE WERE WISE OLD MEN WHO SPENT THEIR LIVES IN THE JEWISH TEMPLE STUDYING SACRED WORKS. MAURICE'S MOTHER'S FATHER HAD BEEN ONE OF THESE SCHOLARS. AS A CHILD, MAURICE THOUGHT HIS GRANDFATHER'S PICTURE LOOKED EXACTLY LIKE GOD.

Maurice's sister, Natalie, was nine when he was born. She had to take care of baby Maurice, or Murray, as he was called. "She had to schlep me everywhere and she hated it," Maurice remembered. Sometimes she would fly into frightening rages. His brother, Jack, was five  years older than him and was his closest friend. The two of them spent a lot of time together in their room, drawing and making models.

Until he was about six, Maurice was sick a lot. Several times he almost died. Once his grandmother tried to save him by following an old Jewish tradition. She dressed him up all in white so the Angel of Death would think he was already an angel, and leave him alone.

While he was sick, he watched the world through his window. One of his earliest memories was of his grandmother opening and closing the window shade for him as if it were a theater curtain. "The window became my movie camera, my television set," he said. "So happy memories are being indoors looking out windows."

He used to draw what he saw through his window, and turn it into stories. Maurice didn't write the stories. That was Jack's job. Maurice illustrated them.

The brothers would perform their stories for guests. Years later, when they were adults, Jack and Maurice Sendak published two books together.

Outside on the street, Maurice became the storyteller. Because he was sick so much, he wasn't good at sports. But he made himself important by telling the other children stories. "I would get them all on the stoop and I would tell them the movie I had seen," he told an interviewer at the Rosenbach Museum. "And then I'd invent parts of the movie, especially gruesomey parts."

Maurice had a lot of movie stories to tell. On Fridays, the local movie theater gave away free dishes. Maurice's mother wanted to collect the whole set of dishes, so they went to the movies every Friday.

The Sendak children didn't have any children's books. Mostly Maurice read comic books. His first real book was a gift from his sister for his ninth birthday. It was a beautiful edition of Mark Twain's *The Prince and the Pauper*. He fell in love with the book—he stared at it for hours. Then he smelled it.

He was used to comic books printed on cheap pulp paper. So to Maurice, this book smelled very elegant. He even tried to bite it. Finally he sat down and read it.

Chapter 2
Nowhere Is Safe

Objects and events from his childhood stayed with Maurice all his life and showed up in his books. Mickey Mouse was born the same year as Maurice. Maurice loved him because he was "brave and sassy and nasty and crooked and thinking of ways to outdo people." There was nothing cute about Mickey. At the movies, a Mickey Mouse short would often be shown before the main movie. Before it started, Maurice's brother and sister knew they should get ready to grab Murray. "When Mickey appeared on the screen, I would stand on my seat and scream," he remembered.

MICKEY MOUSE

MICKEY MOUSE, WALT DISNEY'S MOST FAMOUS CARTOON CHARACTER, FIRST APPEARED ON NOVEMBER 18, 1928, IN *STEAMBOAT WILLIE*. IN THAT MOVIE, MICKEY GOT INTO PLENTY OF TROUBLE. HE GRABBED MINNIE MOUSE BY HER UNDERPANTS WITH A HOOK TO HAUL HER ONTO HIS BOAT. HE TWISTED PIGLETS' TAILS TO TURN THEM INTO MUSICAL INSTRUMENTS. IT WAS THIS WILD, NAUGHTY MOUSE THAT MAURICE FELL IN LOVE WITH. OVER THE YEARS,

DISNEY MADE MICKEY MUCH MORE CUDDLY. AS AN ADULT, MAURICE COLLECTED MICKEY MOUSE ITEMS. HIS HOUSE WAS FULL OF TOYS, BOOKS, AND PRODUCTS SHOWING MICKEY MOUSE. BUT ONLY EARLY ONES. HE THOUGHT THAT, LATER ON, WALT DISNEY HAD MADE MICKEY TOO "PLACID AND NICE AND ADORABLE."

Another early love was music. His sister took him to an outdoor performance of the opera *Carmen*. Halfway through, it started to rain so heavily that the opera had to be cancelled. But he had heard enough to be hooked. He learned to whistle the music of his favorite composers and sing entire operas from memory. He loved Mozart most of all. He thought of him as almost a god. He once said, "I know that if there's a purpose for life, it was for me to hear Mozart."

Other strong memories from his childhood were darker. In 1932, the kidnapping of a baby made headlines across the country. This baby was the son of Charles and Anne Lindbergh. Charles Lindbergh was the first person to fly a plane nonstop across the Atlantic Ocean. He became a world-famous hero. His nickname was Lucky Lindy. The Lindbergh baby was found dead in the woods a few months after the kidnapping.

Even though Maurice was not yet four years old, the story terrified him. The Lindbergh baby was a perfect little American with blond curls and dimples. If a little boy like this wasn't safe, how could the sick child of a poor Polish couple in Brooklyn be safe?

Maurice grew up during the time when Europe was moving toward World War II. Both of Maurice's parents had many Jewish relatives in Poland. The Nazi Party in Germany was taking power. The Nazis wanted to get rid of all the Jews in Europe.

The hatred of Jews—called anti-Semitism—was growing. Villages were attacked. Whole Jewish families were murdered. Maurice's mother sometimes tried to make him behave by reminding him about what had happened to his young relatives in the old country. "If I came up late for dinner," he told NPR interviewer Terry Gross in 2003, "I'd hear about . . . the children who were my age who could never come home for supper and were good to their mothers but now they were dead."

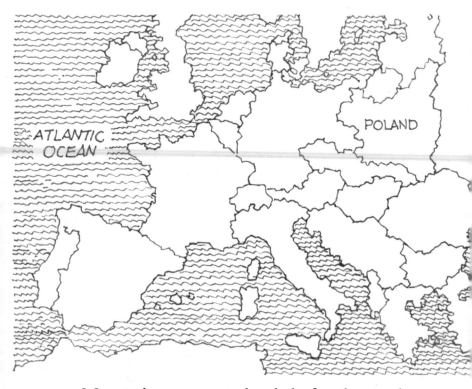

Maurice's parents tried to help family members in Poland escape. They were able to bring some relatives to the United States. But many others did not make it out. On the morning of his bar mitzvah (a special ceremony for Jewish boys when they turn thirteen), Maurice learned that his father's entire village back in Poland had been destroyed by Nazis. Every one of his relatives in Europe had been killed.

From an early age, Maurice knew that terrible things happened in the real world. But most children's books showed the world as a cozy, secure place. When he started to write his own children's books, he decided not to do that. "You learn very quickly that parents can't protect you," he said. "You never feel safe. It's the way I *know* I felt as a child."

Chapter 3
The Young Cartoonist

When he was twelve, Maurice saw Walt Disney's *Fantasia*. This movie is a series of animated stories, including hippo ballerinas and Mickey Mouse as a sorcerer's apprentice. They are all set to classical music. The movie combined his

two favorite things, music and drawing. It excited him so much that he decided to be an illustrator when he grew up.

The only things he enjoyed at school were drawing and reading books in the library. In high school, he drew his own comic strip for the school paper. He also worked after school for All-American Comics. His job was to take popular newspaper comic strips and help make them

into comic books. He drew in backgrounds and filled in missing details. He particularly enjoyed drawing the little puffs of smoke that showed how fast a character was supposed to be running.

In December of 1941, the United States entered World War II. Maurice was in high school. Though all the battles were fought abroad, the war came very close to the Sendak family. Maurice's brother joined the US Army and was, for a while, missing in action. The man his sister

was engaged to also joined the army, and was killed. But Maurice himself never had to become a soldier. He graduated from high school in 1946, a year after the war ended.

By that time, Maurice had already been hired to illustrate his first book. His high school science teacher was working on a textbook called *Atomics for the Millions*. The book tried to make atomic science simple and

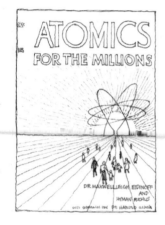

interesting for ordinary readers. So Maurice's teacher invited the young cartoonist to make funny drawings for the book. Maurice came up with scenes from everyday life to help explain atomic reactions. For instance, his illustration shows three girls who represent sodium atoms meeting up with three boys who represent chlorine atoms. When they pair off and begin

dancing together, each couple forms a molecule of salt. In return for his clever drawings, he was paid one hundred dollars, and his teacher gave him a passing grade in science.

Chapter 4
Open Doors

In the days after the war ended, Maurice remembered, anything seemed possible. "Doors opened, and . . . young people were welcomed," he told an interviewer from *The Comics Journal.* "New things were happening, a surge of energy: a surge of hope. A surge of happiness." He found

himself a wonderful job as an artist with a
company that created displays for store windows.
He was living in Manhattan, and working with
other young people who dreamed of being artists.

He remembered this as one of the best times of
his life. He was so good at what he did that he
was promoted. A promotion should be good news.

For Maurice it wasn't. Now he worked with older people who felt stuck in their jobs. Most of them had once hoped to become artists, but none of them had. Maurice found this so depressing that he quit.

Quitting meant moving back in with his parents in Brooklyn. Lonely and unhappy, he went back to a habit from his childhood. He spent

all his time staring out the window, sketching.
He became particularly interested in a little girl
named Rosie. With his window open, he could
hear her talking to the other children. She would
make up games and stories, and bully them
into playing along. Once he heard her gleefully
describing her own grandmother's death in great
detail, until the grandmother herself appeared

on the steps. Another time she described a
fight between her parents, as if she were a radio
announcer. Years later, Rosie would become the
heroine of his book *The Sign on Rosie's Door*.

That summer Jack was also out of work and
living at home. Together, the brothers came
up with an idea to make money. They created
boxes with tiny wooden figures that moved and
acted out scenes from fairy tales. They took
them to FAO Schwarz in Manhattan. It was

the most famous toy store in the world. The buyer there loved the toys. But they were much too complicated to be mass-produced and sold. Still, the buyer was so impressed that he offered Maurice a job creating window displays.

Maurice was happy to be back in Manhattan. He began taking night classes at a school called the Art Students' League. This was the only formal art training he ever had. He spent a lot of time in FAO Schwarz's book section. The woman

in charge of buying books became his friend.
She thought he should try to illustrate children's
books.

Maurice particularly liked the books published
by Harper & Brothers. One day Harper's

children's book editor, Ursula Nordstrom, was expected to visit FAO Schwarz. Maurice's drawings were spread out all over the book department. Maurice said it was "like putting a huge hook in the water and waiting for a fish to be caught."

Chapter 5
Setting Words to Pictures

Maurice caught his fish!

Ursula Nordstrom saw Maurice's drawings, and the next day offered him a job illustrating a book. It was called *The Wonderful Farm,* and it came out in 1951. Maurice's pictures were charming, but nothing special. Maurice didn't yet know how to illustrate a children's book.

He was lucky in his editor. Ursula Nordstrom realized that Maurice Sendak had unusual talent. So she set out to help him learn. She chose books for him to illustrate that would help him find his special skills. The third book she gave him was

A Hole Is to Dig by Ruth Krauss. This was a
kind of children's book that had never been
done before. It was made up of definitions of
words written by children. The definitions were
imaginative. For instance, "Dogs are to kiss
people." The book was a challenge because it
had no story and no characters. Maurice worked

closely on it with the author. He visited her and her husband on their farm in Connecticut so often that he began to call them his "weekend parents."

More than sixty years later, *A Hole Is to Dig* is still in print. The children in the illustrations look different from his earlier drawings. They are square and dark. They look tough and full of fight. This is because Maurice based his characters

URSULA NORDSTROM

MAURICE SENDAK'S EDITOR WAS ONE OF THE GREAT LADIES WHO OVERSAW THE FLOWERING OF CHILDREN'S BOOKS IN THE TWENTIETH CENTURY. SHE BEGAN WORKING AT HARPER'S IN 1936, AND QUICKLY ROSE TO BECOME HEAD OF THEIR CHILDREN'S BOOK DEPARTMENT. WHEN SHE WAS ASKED TO EXPLAIN WHY SHE WAS RIGHT FOR THE JOB, SHE ANSWERED, "WELL, I AM A FORMER CHILD, AND I HAVEN'T FORGOTTEN A THING." SHE WAS FAMOUS FOR THE LONG, HELPFUL LETTERS SHE WROTE HER AUTHORS. SHE WAS ESPECIALLY GOOD AT HELPING DISCOURAGED AUTHORS. SHE IS RESPONSIBLE FOR THE BOOKS OF AUTHORS SUCH AS LAURA INGALLS WILDER, E. B. WHITE, MARGARET WISE BROWN, AND SHEL SILVERSTEIN. AFTER HER DEATH, HER LETTERS WERE PUBLISHED IN A BOOK CALLED *DEAR GENIUS*, WITH A COVER BY MAURICE SENDAK.

on the children he saw out his window. He described them as "just Brooklyn kids, old before their time." They are children who have already learned that life is not easy. From then on, all the children in Maurice's books would look this way. Although he used many different styles over the years, it is always easy to recognize his drawings.

A Hole Is to Dig was so successful that Maurice was able to quit his job and become a full-time illustrator. He was only twenty-four years old.

Over the next five years, Maurice worked hard, illustrating as many as six books in a year. He began to develop his own idea of what a children's book illustrator should do. He didn't want to just show what was happening in the story. He wanted to add something new. "The best-illustrated books," he told a *Comics Journal* interviewer, "are the books where the text does one thing and the pictures say something just a little off-center of the language, so they're both doing something. . . . The most boring books are where the pictures are restating the text."

Even though he didn't have any musical talent, he thought being an illustrator was like being a composer. A composer sets words to music, creating a song that transforms the words into something new and different. In the same way, Maurice said, he was setting words to pictures.

Chapter 6
First Loves and First Books

Maurice decided he was "desperately in need of a dog," so in 1953 he bought Jennie, a white Sealyham terrier. He called her "the love of my life." He drew Jennie into the next  book he illustrated, *Mrs. Piggle-Wiggle's Farm*. As long as Jenny lived, she appeared somewhere in every book he illustrated.

At about the same time, he met the other love of his life, Eugene Glynn. Eugene was a psychiatrist, a doctor who helps people with emotional problems. He had a special interest in working with troubled young people. Maurice and Eugene became a couple. Maurice never told his parents he was gay. He thought  it would make them unhappy. He also kept it a secret from the public. He knew some people wouldn't like knowing that a popular children's illustrator was gay, and it might damage his career. However, he and Eugene were a devoted couple who stayed together for fifty years. They shared a love of reading, art, music, and travel.

Maurice once described an illustrator as "someone who so falls in love with writing that he wishes he had written it." Now, after illustrating more than twenty books written by other people, he decided it was time to try writing his own book. When he was working on other people's books, Maurice always believed that the words came first. Only after a story was finished could the artist come along and add his own part of the story.

He approached his own first book in the same way. Until the text was written, he didn't even think about the pictures. He worked very hard at his writing. He spent the summer of 1955 at a writers' colony in Yelping Hill, Connecticut. His editor, Ursula Nordstrom, came to visit on weekends. She would walk in the woods with him

for hours, helping him figure out what he was trying to say.

Kenny's Window was published in 1956. Kenny has a dream in which a four-legged rooster asks seven questions that Kenny must answer to get into a beautiful garden. The questions are puzzling and dreamlike. For instance, "Can you draw a picture on the blackboard when somebody doesn't want you to?" and "What is an only goat?"

Looking back, Maurice thought that the book showed how much he still had to learn. He thought the text was too long and the pictures were awful. Others did not agree. The book was successful enough to encourage him to write another book, *Very Far Away*. It wasn't until his third book, however, that Maurice really started to write like himself and no one else.

In 1960, he published *The Sign on Rosie's Door*. This book was based on Brooklyn Rosie. He still had two dozen sketchbooks full of drawings, descriptions, and overheard scraps of her conversations. Maurice's Rosie is not a nice child. She is loud, bossy, and vain. She always wants to be the center of attention. But she comes up with wonderful ideas. She saves the other children from their worst enemy on an empty summer day—boredom.

Rosie was one of Maurice's favorite characters. He said that every character he ever created had some of her spirit—what he called "the essential Rosiness of my heroes." Of course there was also a bit of Maurice in Rosie.

Rosie uses her imagination to make the other kids pay attention to her in the same way Maurice had made himself important to the kids on his block by telling them stories.

After Rosie, he wrote the Nutshell Library, a set of four tiny books in a box.

Alligators All Around uses the alphabet to describe the exciting life of a family of alligators. *One Was Johnny* counts from one to ten and back as Johnny has his quiet life invaded by a series of rude visitors. *Chicken Soup with Rice* celebrates the joys of eating soup every month of the year. *Pierre* tells the story of a little boy who just says, "I don't care," to everything, and gets eaten by a lion.

Children immediately loved *The Sign on Rosie's Door* and the Nutshell Library, and they have remained popular ever since.

THE REAL ROSIE

IN 1975, MAURICE COMBINED THE STORY IN *THE SIGN ON ROSIE'S DOOR* AND THE ONES FROM THE NUTSHELL LIBRARY IN AN ANIMATED TV SHOW CALLED *REALLY ROSIE*. THE SONGS AND MUSIC WERE BY THE ROCK MUSICIAN CAROLE KING. MAURICE WENT BACK TO HIS OLD NEIGHBORHOOD TO SHOW THE TV CREW THE BUILDING WHERE ROSIE HAD LIVED. HE KNOCKED ON THE DOOR AND DISCOVERED THAT ROSIE'S COUSIN STILL LIVED THERE. SHE PUT HIM IN TOUCH WITH ROSIE, WHO REMEMBERED THE BOY WHO USED TO WATCH HER FROM HIS WINDOW. FINALLY HE WAS ABLE TO TELL HER THAT ALL THESE YEARS HE HAD BEEN "DRAWING, AND MAKING THINGS UP ABOUT YOU."

THE TV SHOW WAS SO SUCCESSFUL THAT IT BECAME AN OFF-BROADWAY MUSICAL WITH AN ALL-CHILD CAST.

Chapter 7
Wild Things

By 1963, Maurice had written seven books and illustrated more than forty. Five books he illustrated had won Caldecott Honor Medals.

This is an award given every year by librarians to the book that—in their opinion—has the best art. It is one of the highest awards a children's book artist can get. One medal was for a silly book about good manners called *What Do You Say, Dear?* Another was for *Little Bear's Visit*, which was for children first learning to read.

All his books so far were illustrated in only two or three colors. Full-color printing was very expensive. It was much cheaper to print a book in only a few colors. But now Maurice felt ready to do his first full-color book. He came up with what he thought was a poetic title, "Where the Wild Horses Are." But he discovered he simply couldn't draw convincing horses. So his editor asked him what else in his life was wild. He answered, "Relatives."

Maurice's childhood had been full of relatives from Poland. In his memory, they were huge and loud, with bloodshot red eyes, bad teeth, hairy

moles, and long hair growing out of their noses.
They would pinch his cheeks and say, "You're

so cute I could eat you up." Sometimes, when his mother was slow in bringing out dinner, he was afraid they really would eat him up. The relatives spoke Yiddish, a language that Jews of Eastern Europe spoke. In Yiddish, there is a word, *vildechaya,* that describes a child who is being bad. In English it translates to "wild thing." So his wild horses became wild things.

Before he began drawing, Maurice wanted to be sure the words were absolutely perfect. The final story is only 338 words, but he thought about every one of them. Max, a little boy wearing a wolf suit, is causing trouble. His mother sends him to bed without supper. His room becomes a jungle, and he sails away to the land of the Wild Things. He tames them and becomes their king. Eventually he becomes lonely and returns home to discover that his mother has left him his supper.

Maurice always liked to say that *Where the Wild Things Are* was greeted with a storm of disapproval. He was exaggerating. But it is true that it puzzled or worried some adults. Today, their worries seem silly. But that is partly because *Where the Wild*  *Things Are* helped change picture books. Before it came out, most children's books only talked about nice feelings. After *Where the Wild Things Are* was released, people started to realize that it was good for a picture book to deal with other feelings, like anger and fear.

Many adults saw right away that this book was something special. In 1964, it won the Caldecott Medal. Maurice was happy to receive such a great honor. But it pleased him more that children liked his book.

One little boy sent him a fan letter. He sent
back a drawing of a Wild Thing. What a special

thing for a child to keep! But soon after, Maurice got a letter from the boy's mother: "Jim loved your card so much he ate it." Maurice always said this was one of the best compliments he ever received.

Chapter 8
The Night Kitchen

Winning the Caldecott Medal meant that from now on Maurice could choose what books he wanted to work on. One project he loved was *Zlateh the Goat*. This was a selection of stories

by the great Polish American author Isaac Bashevis Singer. The stories take place in a Jewish *shtetl*. Maurice based the characters on photographs of his parents'

Polish relatives who hadn't survived the war. This project impressed Maurice's parents—they thought of Isaac Bashevis Singer as the author of "real

books." It helped convince them that their son was doing important work.

Still, the next few years were very difficult ones. By 1965, his beloved dog, Jennie, was getting old. And his mother had cancer. He

realized they would both die soon. To help deal with his fears, he began working on a book about Jennie. *Higgelty Piggelty Pop!* is the longest book he ever wrote. Jennie decides, "There must be more to life than having everything." So she leaves home. In the end, she writes her old master a letter telling him she is very happy. It begins, "As

you probably noticed, I went away forever." Although the book is about Jennie, Maurice managed to refer to his mother as well. One picture is copied from a photograph of baby Maurice in his mother's arms.

The month after *Higgelty Piggelty Pop!* appeared, Jennie died. A year later, in 1968, his mother died. His father moved into Maurice's small apartment in New York. Maurice convinced his father to try writing down some of the stories he used to tell his children. These stories were later

published as *In Grandpa's House*, with illustrations by Maurice Sendak. In 1970, two years after his mother's death, his father died as well.

All through this sad time, Maurice was working on his most personal book, *In the Night Kitchen*, which is dedicated to his parents. The story grew from a childhood memory of the 1939 World's Fair in New York. Because eleven-year-old

Maurice was too young to go alone, his parents
had made Natalie and her boyfriend take him.

One attraction at the fair was the Sunshine
Bakery. Their slogan was, "We Bake While You
Sleep!" Young Maurice thought this was terribly
unfair. He wanted to see the baking done! He
used to save their coupons, which showed "three

fat little Sunshine bakers going off to this magic place at night, wherever it was, to have their fun, while I had to go to bed," he told author Jonathan Cott. At the bakery in the fairgrounds, men dressed as bakers came out and waved at the crowd.

Maurice was enchanted. He didn't realize that Natalie and her boyfriend had sneaked off, leaving him all alone. Even though being lost was scary,

Maurice was thrilled. The police took him home in a car with the sirens going. And his sister got in trouble. He said that he'd written *In the Night Kitchen* "to say that I am now old enough to stay up at night and know what's happening in the Night Kitchen!"

He threw into the book all the things he had loved as a child. The hero of the book is named Mickey, after his favorite, Mickey Mouse.

NEW YORK WORLD'S FAIR

THE NEW YORK WORLD'S FAIR THAT INSPIRED *IN THE NIGHT KITCHEN* BILLED ITSELF AS THE "WORLD OF TOMORROW." ALL KINDS OF NEW AND EXCITING TECHNOLOGY COULD BE SEEN AT THE FAIR. PRESIDENT FRANKLIN D. ROOSEVELT'S OPENING-DAY SPEECH WAS TELEVISED, EVEN THOUGH TV WAS STILL SO NEW THAT THERE WERE ONLY TWO HUNDRED TELEVISION SETS IN ALL OF NEW YORK CITY TO WATCH IT ON. FAIRGOERS COULD VIEW A HUGE MODEL SHOWING THE CITY OF THE FUTURE. THERE WERE ALL SORTS OF GADGETS TO MAKE LIFE EASIER. MAURICE RECALLED SOME OF ITS ENERGY, EXCITEMENT, AND SENSORY OVERLOAD IN HIS ARTWORK FOR *IN THE NIGHT KITCHEN.*

The three bakers all look like Oliver Hardy, a famous movie comedian. The style of the art is based on the comic books that Maurice had loved best. Jennie's name appears several times. There are also references to his  parents, his birthday, and Eugene. The skyline of the night city is based on the New York skyline that he used to look at longingly from Brooklyn. It is made entirely of food containers. Whenever his sister took him to the city, the first thing they did was go to a restaurant. "To me, New York represented eating," Maurice said. So the book is full of the pleasures of food.

The book is also full of the terrors of his childhood. Little Mickey is all alone in the Night Kitchen, just as Maurice had been at the World's

Fair. The bakers are scary figures who threaten to bake Mickey into their bread. But, like Max in *Where the Wild Things Are*, Mickey is not afraid of anything, and he comes out on top.

Maurice said that this book was his favorite because it came "from the direct middle of me." Once again, critics objected—but for a reason that took Maurice by surprise. Mickey falls "out of his clothes" and into the Night Kitchen. So of course, at the beginning of the book, he is naked. Maurice liked to refer to one picture as a "frontal nudie."

People thought this made it a dirty book. Some librarians drew or pasted diapers onto Mickey before they were willing to put the book on the shelves. Even today, *In the Night Kitchen* is on the list of books most often challenged or banned in libraries. Fortunately, the scandal of little naked Mickey did not stop children from loving the story. And in 1971, the book was awarded a Caldecott Honor Medal.

CENSORSHIP

PEOPLE WILL ALWAYS
DISAGREE ABOUT WHICH
SUBJECTS ARE PROPER
FOR CHILDREN'S BOOKS.
SOME PEOPLE WANT TO
HAVE THE BOOKS THEY
DON'T APPROVE OF
BANNED. THIS MEANS
THAT THEY WOULD NOT
BE ALLOWED TO BE USED IN

LIBRARIES OR SCHOOLS. THE AMERICAN LIBRARY
ASSOCIATION KEEPS TRACK OF ATTEMPTS TO TAKE
BOOKS—EVERYTHING FROM *LITTLE RED RIDING HOOD*
TO HARRY POTTER—OUT OF READERS' HANDS.
WHEN LIBRARIANS PUT DIAPERS ON MAURICE
SENDAK'S MICKEY, THEY WEREN'T ALLOWING
THE PUBLIC TO SEE THE BOOK AS MAURICE
HAD CREATED IT. MAURICE'S EDITOR, URSULA
NORDSTROM, WROTE A POWERFUL LETTER TO
LIBRARIANS AND PUBLISHERS EXPLAINING WHY
SHE OPPOSED THIS AND ASKING FOR THEIR
SUPPORT.

Chapter 9
Outside

In 1967, while he was in England, Maurice suffered a serious heart attack and almost died. He was only thirty-nine years old. He began to think he needed to live someplace calmer than New York City. Eventually he found a farmhouse in the Connecticut countryside. He fell in love with it

on sight. In 1972, he and Eugene moved there. He hired a local girl to help around the house. Her name was Lynn Caponera. Lynn would stay with Maurice for the rest of his life.

Maurice still missed Jennie terribly. Now he thought it was finally time to get another dog. He couldn't bear to get another Sealyham terrier

like Jennie. So he picked a golden retriever puppy named Io. Soon after, he got a German shepherd named Erda. Although he loved his new dogs, he had trouble with them. They were much bigger than Jennie, and—he thought—not as intelligent. He had a weak heart, and when the big dogs tried to run and pull him along with them, it frightened Maurice.

A man named Matthew Margolis helped Maurice train the dogs. They became friends, and Maurice and Matthew wrote a book together called *Some Swell Pup, or Are You Sure You Want a Dog?* Once again, the book got Maurice in trouble with reviewers, this time because he showed that young puppies poop on the floor.

Maurice settled contentedly into his house in the country. His life was quiet and uneventful. "I want to be alone and work until the day my head hits the drawing table and I'm dead," he once said. For the next forty years, that is pretty much what his life was like. He stayed at home and worked.

His next book would take him a year and a half, and more than one hundred drafts, to write.

He thought of this book, *Outside Over There*, as part of a trilogy— three books that belong together. In Maurice's trilogy, the other two

books were *Where the Wild Things Are* and *In the Night Kitchen.* The stories and characters in the three books are very different, but they all draw very deeply on feelings from his childhood.

"The last part of my trilogy is going to be the strangest," Maurice told an interviewer. And it is. A young girl named Ida is supposed to be minding her baby sister, who is snatched away by goblins. Maurice described the story as coming to him in bits and pieces. The first lines suddenly floated into his head, he said, and "I'm not even sure I know what they mean."

The book grew out of an earlier project. In 1971, he had walked all over Germany gathering material for a collection of Grimms' fairy tales, called *The Juniper Tree.* One story haunted him. It described

the way goblins would steal a baby away if its mother wasn't watching. They would leave a changeling—a substitute baby made of ice. This story reminded him of the way his sister had hated looking after him when he was a baby. Maybe she had sometimes wished goblins would take him away.

It also made him think of the kidnapping of the Lindbergh baby. The fear this had raised in him had never completely left him. In *Outside Over There*, published in 1981, Maurice finally put this fear to rest. Ida is based on his sister, Natalie. In one picture, the baby's face is an exact copy of the Lindbergh baby's. "I was trying to change history," he told *The Horn Book*'s Roger Sutton. "Ida finds the baby. I refused to let the Lindbergh baby die."

Outside Over There wasn't as popular as the other two books in the trilogy. Perhaps it made readers uncomfortable to experience jealousy and insecurity so strongly. But Maurice had achieved exactly what he wanted to. *"Outside Over There,"* he declared, "is a wonderful book." The book earned him another Caldecott Honor.

Chapter 10
Opera

Maurice called writing *Outside Over There* "the most painful experience of my creative life." Halfway through, he almost gave up on the book altogether. Instead, he turned to another art form. All his life, he had worshipped music. He was not himself a musician. However, working in opera, he could make use of his talents as an artist.

In 1975, he had started working on an opera based on *Where the Wild Things Are* with composer Oliver Knussen. Maurice's job was to write the libretto (the words) and design the sets and costumes. Creating a new opera is very slow work. *Where the Wild Things Are* was still not finished when, in 1978, Maurice got an unexpected phone call. Opera director Frank Corsaro had fallen in love with Maurice's illustrations for the Grimms' fairy tales. He wondered if Maurice would be interested in designing a production of Mozart's *The Magic Flute*. It would be performed by the Houston Opera.

WOLFGANG AMADEUS MOZART

Maurice adored Mozart's music, especially *The Magic Flute*. He even put Mozart into the illustrations for *Outside Over There*. (Because that story was so full of menace, he wanted

Mozart to watch over his characters.) Being asked to work on this particular opera just when he was so upset by his book was, he said, "sort of a miracle."

The Magic Flute is a fairy-tale story, with dragons, dancing animals, and a bird catcher dressed in feathers. Maurice approached it as a story about children coming of age. The main characters, Pamina and Tamino, are helped by three little boy spirits. These characters can always be trusted. Maurice believed that "Mozart

is saying, the only people that live in this world who don't lie are children." Maurice's *The Magic Flute* opened on November 14, 1980. People loved it. Several other opera companies borrowed the production, so that many people could see Maurice's vision of Mozart.

The opera for *Where the Wild Things Are* was not such a success. In 1980, it was ready for a trial production. Only two weeks after *The Magic Flute* opened, *Where the Wild Things Are* was performed in Brussels, Belgium. The first show, Maurice said, was "ghastly." A large part of the problem was the costumes. They were hot and heavy, and the singers had trouble seeing in them. "The kids who came to see it just loved to see a Wild Thing fall down," Maurice remembered. One even fell into the orchestra pit. A revised version was more successful. A few years later, Maurice and the composer collaborated again on an operatic version of *Higgelty Piggelty Pop!*

Maurice was hooked. For the next thirty years, he spent much more time designing other opera productions than he did illustrating books. He also designed one ballet, the Christmas story *The Nutcracker*. "I'll go back to books, of course," he said, but "I have started a new career." What he most enjoyed about the theater was the chance

to work with other people. He called working on books "solitary confinement." In the theater, he said, "you're with crazy people, but they're wonderful. It's very sociable."

Chapter 11
Old Fears

During his opera years, Maurice worked only on books that were special to him. In 1983, a long-lost letter was found. It had been written by Wilhelm Grimm, one of the Brothers Grimm famous for their fairy tales. In this letter to a little girl named Mili, Wilhelm told an original story. Maurice's 1988 illustrated version of this fairy tale, *Dear Mili*, was a best seller not only on children's book lists but also on adult best-seller lists.

In 1990, the seed of another book grew from a terrible image that Maurice could not get out of his mind. On one of the most expensive and elegant shopping streets in Los Angeles, Maurice saw the dirty foot of a homeless child sticking out of a cardboard box. He turned this image into his next book, *We Are All in the Dumps with Jack and Guy.*

It is one of his most surreal books. Maurice used images and words from two nonsensical nursery rhymes to create a tale about a group of homeless children who rescue a baby from evil rats. Once again, the book divided critics. Some thought children would be puzzled, upset, or just bored. Others guessed that children would understand what Maurice was saying much better than their parents did.

Maurice's next important book came directly from his work in opera, and from his childhood memories of the terrors of the Holocaust, during

which the Nazis had murdered millions of Jews. In 2000, a friend sent him a recording of *Brundibar*, a children's opera by Hans Krása.

The opera was supposed to have been performed in 1942 by a cast of children from a Jewish orphanage in Prague. However, before it could

take place, the conductor and most of the children in the cast were sent to the Nazi concentration camp of Terezín. There Krása reconstructed the score of the opera from memory, and it was performed fifty-five times by a cast of children in the camp.

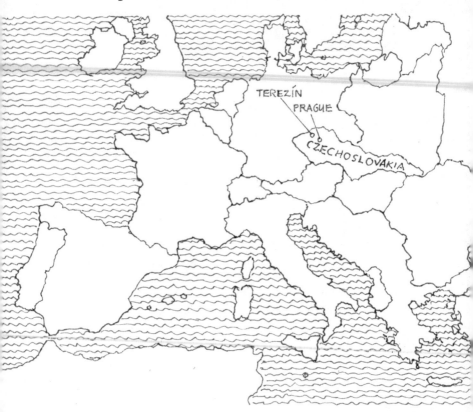

TEREZÍN
PRAGUE
CZECHOSLOVAKIA

Maurice asked his friend Tony Kushner to write an English version of the libretto and also to adapt the text for a picture book. *Brundibar* is a simple folktale about two children whose mother is sick. When they try to sing in the marketplace to earn money for milk to cure her, they are prevented by Brundibar, a powerful bully. Other children and animals join with them to frighten Brundibar away, and they are able to earn the milk to cure their mother.

Maurice wasn't sure how far to go in showing the similarities between Brundibar and the Nazi leader Adolf Hitler. At first he drew Brundibar as Hitler, but that approach seemed out of place in a folktale. So he redrew him as a teenage thug with a little mustache like Hitler's.

THE HOLOCAUST

IN THE 1930S AND '40S, THE NAZIS, LED BY
ADOLF HITLER, TRIED TO WIPE OUT ALL THE
JEWS OF EUROPE. JEWS WERE HERDED INTO
CONCENTRATION CAMPS AND THEN KILLED. THIS
MASS MURDER IS NOW CALLED THE HOLOCAUST.
MAURICE'S PICTURE BOOK *BRUNDIBAR* NEVER
DIRECTLY MENTIONS THE HOLOCAUST, OR TEREZÍN,
THE CONCENTRATION CAMP WHERE THE OPERA
WAS FIRST PERFORMED. HOWEVER, DETAILS IN
THE ART HINT AT THE BACKGROUND OF THE STORY.
FOR EXAMPLE, SOME CHILDREN WEAR YELLOW
STARS ON THEIR CLOTHES. THE NAZIS MADE ALL
JEWS DO THIS.

ALTHOUGH THOUSANDS OF PEOPLE DIED IN
TEREZÍN, THE NAZIS PRETENDED THAT IT WAS
ACTUALLY A NEW HOMETOWN HITLER WAS GIVING
THE JEWISH PEOPLE. PLAYS, MUSIC, AND ART
WERE ALLOWED IN THE CAMP, BECAUSE THE NAZIS
COULD USE THIS AS PROOF OF HOW WELL THEY
WERE TREATING THE JEWS. A PERFORMANCE OF
BRUNDIBAR IN TEREZÍN WAS SHOWN TO THE RED
CROSS. ITS CAST WAS ALL CHILDREN. VIEWERS
DID NOT KNOW THAT AFTER PERFORMANCES OF
THE OPERA, NEW SINGERS HAD TO BE CAST, AS
MEMBERS OF THE OLD CAST WERE SENT TO A
DEATH CAMP.

The ending of *Brundibar* seemed a little too happy. Maurice knew it was not so easy to defeat evil. So in the book, after the story ends, there is one more page with a note from Brundibar: "They believe they've won the fight, they believe I'm gone—not quite! . . . Though I go, I won't go far—I'll be back."

Earlier, Maurice had put his fears about the Lindbergh baby to rest by writing *Outside Over There*. Now, with the publication of *Brundibar* in 2003, he finally dealt directly with the other great terror of his childhood—the Holocaust. "It sort of rounds out my life," he said.

Chapter 12
Through the Picture

In some ways, Maurice enjoyed old age. He no longer cared what other people thought of him. In interviews, he stated exactly what he thought. If he hated someone, or thought something was stupid, he said so.

However, the people he loved were also getting old. His brother died in 1995. His sister died in 2004. Then Eugene, whom he had been with for fifty years, got lung cancer. Maurice set up the house in Connecticut so that he and Lynn Caponera could care for him there. Eugene died in 2007.

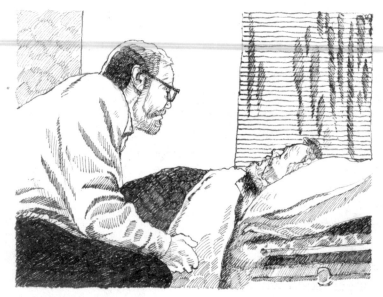

Maurice needed a challenge to distract him during this painful time. He had not both written and illustrated a book since *Outside Over There,*

almost thirty years earlier. Now he decided to try again.

Back in the 1970s, Maurice had created two animated short films for the children's television show *Sesame Street*. One told the story of a boy named Bumble-Ardy who gave a party. Maurice decided his new book would use his film's basic story line and the same rhymes. But it became much darker. Bumble-Ardy is a pig whose parents never let him have a birthday party. After his parents are made into bacon and eaten, he is adopted by his aunt. He throws himself a ninth birthday party, which is such a disaster that he tells his aunt, "I promise, I swear, I won't ever turn ten."

Bumble-Ardy came out in 2011. It was the last book to appear during Maurice's lifetime.

He left one book unfinished, a poem dedicated to Jack, called *My Brother's Book*.

Ever since Eugene's death, Maurice had begun to feel that his own life was coming to a close. And he was ready.

When Maurice was a small child, a picture of his dead grandfather hung over his bed. One day his mother came in to find him trying to climb into the picture. He had a high fever and was speaking in Yiddish. His grandfather had spoken Yiddish, but little Maurice didn't know how to speak the language.

His mother thought her father's ghost was trying to lure her son into the spirit world. To stop him, she tore the picture into little pieces. Years later, Maurice found them. He took the pieces to the Metropolitan Museum of Art, where someone spent months putting them back together. From then on, the picture hung over Maurice's bed.

Someday, he told people, "I'm going to go through the picture."

On May 8, 2012, he did. Although his death saddened the world, Maurice Sendak was now Outside Over There, in the Night Kitchen, Where the Wild Things Are.

TIMELINE OF
MAURICE SENDAK'S LIFE

1928	Born on June 10 in Brooklyn, New York
1947	Illustrates his first book, *Atomics for the Millions*
1950	Meets editor Ursula Nordstrom
1951	Illustrates his first children's book, *The Wonderful Farm* by Marcel Aymé
1956	*Kenny's Window* is published
1963	*Where the Wild Things Are* is published
1967	Suffers a heart attack His beloved dog, Jennie, dies
1968	His mother, Sarah, dies of cancer
1970	Wins international Hans Christian Andersen Award Father, Philip, dies *In the Night Kitchen* is published
1972	Moves from New York to Connecticut
1979	Designs sets for the opera *Where the Wild Things Are*
1981	*Outside Over There* is published
1996	Receives the National Medal of Arts from President Clinton
2003	*Brundibar* is published
2007	Dr. Eugene Glynn dies
2011	*Bumble Ardy* is published
2012	Dies on May 8

TIMELINE OF THE WORLD

Mickey Mouse stars in his first cartoon	1928
Charles Lindbergh's baby is kidnapped	1932
New York World's Fair opens in April / World War II begins	1939
The children's opera *Brundibar* is performed in Terezín, a concentration camp in Czechoslovakia	1943
World War II ends	1945
New Yorkers Julius and Ethel Rosenberg are executed for spying for the Soviet Union	1953
Dr. Seuss's *The Cat in the Hat* is published	1957
The German Democratic Republic begins building the Berlin Wall	1961
Neil Armstrong walks on the moon	1969
A never-before-published story by Wilhelm Grimm is discovered	1983
Editor Ursula Nordstrom dies	1988
The Berlin Wall falls	1989
First e-book reader is introduced. Maurice Sendak hates it	1998
The World Trade Center and the Pentagon are attacked by al-Qaeda on September 11	2001
Barack Obama elected the first African American president of the United States	2008

BIBLIOGRAPHY

Bangs, Lance and Spike Jonze. **Tell Them Anything You Want: A Portrait of Maurice Sendak**. DVD. Oscilloscope Laboratories, 2010.

Cott, Jonathan. **Pipers at the Gates of Dawn: The Wisdom of Children's Literature**. Random House, New York, 1983.

Fresh Air. "Fresh Air Remembers Author Maurice Sendak." May 8, 2012. Mixed media, including interviews of Maurice Sendak by Terry Gross from 1989, 1993, 2003, 2009, and 2011. http://www.npr.org/2012/05/08/152248901/fresh-air-remembers-author-maurice-sendak.

Groth, Gary. "Maurice Sendak Interview Sneak Preview." **The Comics Journal**, May 10, 2012. Archived at http://www.tcj.com/maurice-sendak-interview-sneak-preview/.

Horn Book, The. "Maurice Sendak, 1928-2012." May 8, 2012. Archived at http://www.hbook.com/2012/05/news/obituaries-news/maurice-sendak-1928-2012/.

Kushner, Tony. **The Art of Maurice Sendak: 1980 to the Present**. Abrams, New York, 2003.

Lanes, Selma G. **The Art of Maurice Sendak**. Abrams, New York, 1980.

Sendak, Maurice. **Caldecott & Co.: Notes on Books & Pictures.** Farrar, Straus and Giroux, New York, 1988.

Sendak, Maurice. "Maurice Sendak: Where the Wild Things Are." Interview by Bill Moyers. **NOW with Bill Moyers.** March 12, 2004. Transcript at http://www.pbs.org/now/thisweek/index_031204.html.

Sendak, Maurice. "Sendak." Interviews from the Maurice Sendak Collection, Rosenbach Museum and Library. http://www.livestream.com/rosenbach/folder?dirId=e10bfb24-888c-4466-a2f2-461c7097cb82.